I'M A CHILD...LOVE ME!

Written by Denise Angelle

Illustrations by Isaac Kwesi Arthur

ISBN 978-0-9809403-5-0
Comfort-Heed Publications
A Division of WORLDSTRENGTH

I AM

ONE OF

GOD'S GREAT

MIRACLES!

I'M A CHILD...LOVE ME!

GOD SAYS HE KNEW ME

BEFORE I WAS

KNIT TOGETHER

IN MY MOTHER'S WOMB

AND HE CHOSE ME

BEFORE I WAS BORN.

HE PLANNED ME
AND HAS A
GOOD PURPOSE
FOR MY LIFE.

I'M A CHILD...LOVE ME!

GOD SAYS I AM
FEARFULLY AND
WONDERFULLY MADE.
IN FACT, I'M THE
ONLY ONE HE MADE
THAT'S JUST LIKE ME!

HE TOOK HIS TIME

AND SKILLS

TO CREATE

AND PERFECT ME

JUST THE WAY

HE WANTED ME.

I'M A CHILD...

LOVE ME!

THE BIBLE SAYS
THAT CHILDREN
ARE A BLESSING
AND A GIFT
FROM GOD.

JESUS SAID

TO LET THE LITTLE CHILDREN

COME TO HIM

AND DO NOT FORBID THEM

FOR OF SUCH IS THE

KINGDOM OF GOD!

I'M A CHILD...LOVE ME!

AND WHOEVER RECEIVES

A LITTLE CHILD

IN JESUS'S NAME

RECEIVES JESUS

AND GOD WHO SENT HIM.

JESUS ALSO SAID

EVERYONE MUST

RECEIVE THE

KINGDOM OF GOD

AS A LITTLE CHILD DOES.

WE REALLY ARE PRECIOUS

IN HIS SIGHT!

I'M A CHILD...

LOVE ME!

SO PARENTS PLEASE,

TRAIN ME UP IN THE WAY

I SHOULD GO

AND TALK ABOUT

THE WORD OF GOD

WITH ME EVERY DAY.

AND TEACH ME

HIS WAYS AND TRUTH.

THE BIBLE SAYS

THEN WHEN I'M OLD

I WILL NOT

DEPART FROM IT.

I'M A CHILD...LOVE ME!

TAKE THE TIME TO

TREASURE ME,

CARE FOR ME,

COMFORT ME,

PROTECT ME,

PRAY WITH ME,

INSTRUCT ME,

CORRECT ME,

ENJOY ME,

GET TO KNOW ME

AND BE A GOOD

ROLE MODEL FOR ME.

AND MOST OF ALL,

I'M A CHILD...

LOVE ME!

DENISE ANGELLE IS A WRITER, PHOTOGRAPHER, ARTIST, EDUCATOR, HUMANITARIAN AID, HEALTHCARE/SOCIAL ADVOCATE & MISSION DIRECTOR WITH WORLDSTRENGTH. SHE WAS STATIONED IN GHANA, AFRICA DURING THE CREATION OF THIS AFRICA ARISE EDITION OF HER BOOK, "I'M A CHILD...LOVE ME!"

ISAAC KWESI ARTHUR IS AN ARTIST & BIBLE COLLEGE STUDENT FROM GHANA, AFRICA. WITH ISAAC ARE HIS ART STUDENTS, LITTLE DR. KWAME BOAZ AND REBECCA RUTH. WITH GOD'S HELP WORLDSTRENGTH MISSIONS RESCUED THEM FROM MALNUTRITION, DISEASE, NEGLECT & ABUSE. THEY ARE TWO OF THE MANY CHILDREN WE LOVE IN AFRICA!

THIS BOOK
BELONGS TO:

GOD LOVES YOU!

www.ingramcontent.com/pod-product-compliance
Lightning Source LLC
Chambersburg PA
CBHW042137030726
47599CB00002B/508